Of Water Lilies and Warm Hearts

*The time may come
when all you want to do
is be the flower that you are.*

Of Water Lilies and Warm Hearts

Poems to Soothe the Soul
by Nanna Aida Svendsen

Copyright Nanna Svendsen © 2008
First published in 2008 by Pleasant House Ltd
BM Box 6100, Monomark House
27 Old Gloucester Street, London WC1N 3XX
www.pleasanthouse.com

Distributed by Gardners Books, 1 Whittle Drive, Eastbourne, East Sussex, BN23 6QH

The right of Nanna Svendsen to be identified as the author of the work has been asserted herein in accordance with the Copyright, Designs and Patents Act 1988.

All rights reserved. This book is sold subject to the condition that it shall not, by way of trade or otherwise, be lent, resold, hired out or otherwise circulated without the publisher's prior consent in any form of binding or cover other than that in which it is published and without a similar condition including this condition being imposed on the subsequent purchaser.

British Library Cataloguing in Publication Data
A catalogue record for this book is available from the British Library.

ISBN 978-0-9555080-0-4

Typeset by Amolibros, Milverton, Somerset
www.amolibros.com
This book production has been managed by Amolibros
Printed and bound by T J International Ltd, Padstow, Cornwall, UK

'*Waterlilies and Warm Hearts*—what can I say? Your poems help us reach inside ourselves to our essence. They help us remember who we are. They are fierce with tenderness, truth, and love.'

Christiane Northrup MD, *New York Times* Best selling author of *Women's Bodies, Women's Wisdom; The Wisdom of Menopause; Mother Daughter Wisdom*. Noted visionary, speaker and television personality.

'I love reading your poems. They always return me to a heart-centered place immediately.'

Cheryl Richardson, author of the *New York Times* bestselling books, *Take Time for Your Life, Life Makeovers, Stand Up for Your Life* and *The Unmistakable Touch of Grace*. Life coach, presenter, producer and broadcaster.

Water Lilies and Warm Hearts
Nanna Aida Svendsen

About the Book

The water lily has long been seen as a symbol of unfolding consciousness, the heart as a symbol of feelings. These poems speak of a quest to bring awareness to the heart, marry consciousness with feeling, and invite a sense of freedom and compassion to flower. This is a journey blessed with beauty and with pain. How can it be otherwise, when it is of life itself?—of love, loss, longing, and of regaining something essential. Of melding vulnerability with wisdom and becoming ever more ensouled.

About Nanna Aida Svendsen

Nanna Aida Svendsen has more than thirty years experience in the human potential field as an explorer, workshop leader and writer. Her book, a fairy tale, *Freya And the Magic Cloak* was published in 2002, and her writing and poetry have been shared and appreciated internationally.

Whatever the terrain she has been travelling, Nanna has found inspiration and succour from the realms of depth psychology, meditation and the work of the mystic poets. Being in nature has also played a part. Its beauty continues to nourish her daily and a sense of communion with its rhythms and seasons helps her know she belongs.

Born in Britain, Nanna Aida grew up in Denmark and has lived in England, Scandinavia, Spain and the United States. This has helped to deepen her cross-cultural awareness, along with her sensitivity to the influence of surroundings. She feels grateful to the people and places that have helped inspire and inform her writing.

More information about her work may be garnered from her website:
<www.pleasanthouse.com>.

For my water lily sister Cha
Carl and Christopher
Christine and Jody

In memory of Hennie and Jorgen

All my love
Ever and always
Nanna

Contents

Acknowledgements xvii
Prologue xix

The Flower That You Are
      Poems of inhabiting our lives.
      Of finding and living what we love.

Lily of the Deep 3
Listen Deeply 4
Will You 6
When Angels Dream 8
Love Yourself 10
Do You Have the Courage? 12
Soul-work 14
Heart on the Mend 15
You Can Forget 16
Live What You Love 18
An Unacknowledged Grief 19
Lay Your Burden Down 20
Natural Beauty 22
When in Doubt 23
Many Are the Voices 24

The Call 26
The Time Has Come 28
What Is It? 30
The Flower That You Are 32

Moon out of Bounds
> Poems of insecurity and descent. Of finding and honouring lunar aspects of ourselves.

Moon out of Bounds 35
A Time for Retreat 36
In Praise of Acceptance 37
Be Happy? 38
A Welcome Present 39
On the Right Track 40
When 41
Falling Down 42
Oh To Be Understood 44
Circle of Forgiveness 46
Determined Gentleness 47
What Would It Be Like? 48
What To Do? 50
There Is Nothing Like a Friend 52
Crone 53
Moon Woman 54

Woman in Winter
> Poems of a journey through winter. Of being in transition, of opening to feelings, the creative process, and of finding and cherishing the family within.

Being in Winter	59
Winter Heart	60
Not Enough Ink	61
Anxious and Forsaken	62
Skater in the Mist	63
Tender Relating	64
Return to Innocence	66
Time to Reconnect	70
Inner Children	72
Family Within	74
In Transition	79
Back to This Land	80
Cellular Shock	82
False Light	83
City Rose	84
An Ancient Issue	85
Glamour of the Shield	88
Hidden from View	90
Damp Wood on the Fire	92
Last Remnant of the Rain	94

The Smallest Thing 95
Winter Swans 96
Song of the Inlet 98
Edge of Spring 99

Woman in Summer
    Poems of a journey through summer. Of finding new ways of relating, of letting go and trusting, of cycles of death and rebirth.

Pure Spun Gold 103
Morning Reflection 104
Reply to a Worried Mind 105
Tears of Salt 106
It Is Always Like This 108
On The Rise 109
Reply to Mr Cut and Dried 110
In the Mirror 112
All They Did Was Shout 113
A Gift from Existence 116
Mutuality Is Round 118
In a Small Circle 122
Sea of Consciousness 125
Although You Are Gone 126
Sacrifice 128
Black 130
In the Balance 131

Water Lily Hearts
    Poems of connecting with the present. Of longing and belonging, of leaving and of coming home and of remembering the heart.

In Soft Surrender	135
The Gift of Here	136
Whenever I Am Away	138
Longing	139
Longing and Belonging	140
Lost in Transition	141
Cross Cultural Souls	142
Via Negativa. Via Positiva	144
If You Don't Feel Safe	146
Water Lily Heart	149
Being Essential	152
The Road Home	153

Acknowledgements

Warm blessings and thanks go to my dear friends. Over the years you have truly been companions of the heart. The terrain, both inner and outer, that we have travelled together has contributed much to this work. I am eternally grateful to you. Being in your presence soothes my soul. My heart also warms when I think of my family.

Of Water Lilies and Warm Hearts has evolved through many incarnations. I have been blessed in that a number of my friends are also gifted writers and editors. I am thankful for your feedback and support over the years. This work would not have been the same without you. So too the writers' groups I have been a part of. Many thanks also go to the women of Soul Time for the chance to share some of the poems.

I wish to thank writers' coach Julia McCutchen for her support and Jane Tatam of Amolibros for her exquisite care in helping me turn a manuscript into this book.

Special thanks go to Punit Krejsgaard, who with tender loving consideration has helped edit this work, checking its accuracy as to the inner life, and encouraging the constant expressing and mirroring of the heart. You have truly befriended my soul throughout this endeavour and brought much joy to the process.

Great gratitude goes as ever to my beloved husband and soul mate, Carl Lindstrom, whose wise and warm presence fills each day with delight and from whom I learn so much.

Prologue

It is early. I am a little woozy from not enough sleep. Something unknown has kept me restless all night, and has finally wrested me from bed, this cold December dawn—this morning of celebrating Sancta Lucia—bringer of light to the dark season in Sweden.

I sit at a table by a window wrapped in a rug, warming my hands on a hot cup of tea. Looking out into the black morning, I see nothing but the reflection in the glass of a solitary candle placed on the sill. The longed-for snow has not come. A rough rain is flinging itself on the pane instead. Sighing, I take a swig of tea and then, cup poised mid-air, come to a standstill.

Suddenly an idea has come, to assemble a collection of poems mapping a quest to understand and cherish the heart. To link consciousness with feeling, and open, or rather surrender, perhaps, to essence. To distill years of work, pare it down, to the essential, including insights, questions, suggestions and reflections that have come knocking on my door, begging to be recognised, written down and shared.

It seems fitting that an idea such as this should come on this day of celebrating Lucia—of remembering the grace to be found in the darkness.

It's now eight a.m. A solitary candle still burns on the sill and the sun has not yet offered more than a glint upon the sky as, putting down the cup, I reach for paper and pen and begin to write:

Handbook of the Heart
Poems to Soothe the Soul
in Trying Times...

Apparently on that cold December day, when I first wrote those words, I was not ready for the title *Of Water Lilies and Warm Hearts* to present itself to me. A number of winters were to pass. I was to travel deeper into the heart's terrain, further connect with the essential, write many a poem, before it was willing to be revealed.

Nanna Aida Svendsen
Spring 2008

The Flower That You Are

*Poems of inhabiting our lives.
Of finding and living
what we love.*

Lily of the Deep

a water lily drifts upon a pond
rooted in the dark and sustained by the deep
it opens petals in a dance with existence
when a tender light comes
to shine upon it

Listen Deeply

Listen deeply
to the soft voice
of your soul.
It knows who
you are.
Even when lonely
how intimately
you belong.

Its wisdom resounds
beneath the nagging
of your shame, guilt and fear.

The tender presence
of your core brings solace
when needed,
a sense of rightness
when remembered,
communion when close.

The sound
of your original voice
calls you to essence
over and over again,
sometimes with such
vital vulnerability
you would weep.
Sometimes with such
fiery ferocity you would cry.

Sometimes with such softness
it calls for your surrender.

Yes,
listen deeply
to the gifted grace
of your soul.

And in the listening
may the beauty
of your life
be revealed.

Will You

Will you be still?
Quiet, gentle,
Undisturbed,
Present and receptive
Like a silent sea.

And in that silence
Will you stop
The ancient game
Of shame?
Of nagging on yourself
And others?
Or mindless doing
Of the unessential?

And in that stopping
Will you plumb?
Find alignment
With existence
In the deep?

Will you reverberate
With Gaia,
Turning on her axis?
With moons
Circling their planets?
Stars,
Spiralling in their galaxies?

Will you trust
The whispered voice
That lets you know
How profoundly
You belong?

Will you be still

And in that stillness
Allay the agitation
Of the world?

When Angels Dream

Quit everything, dear one
That does not bring you joy
That would ask you to strain
Against yourself.

Let yourself fall
Lovingly
Into your own embrace.
Linger there
Cocooned like some cherub
Wings folded about you.

This is not a time for flight.
This is a time to hunker down
Huddle into the earth
As she warms you with
Her presence
As you warm her with
Your love.

If only you knew how much work
You do every day
How much is transformed
Through your being
You would rest
Knowing you are already
Doing what you must.
Have already done more than enough.

Yes, cherub-like, you wait
Wings folded about you
Changing the world as you dream
Until it is time again to take to the sky.

Love Yourself

Love yourself
As though you were your child

Give yourself
The listening, the mirroring,
The tenderness, the patience

The presence you would
If you were not so afraid

If you did not think
You had to school
To manipulate, shame and should

Or do the very thing
That stopped you
Loving you
In the first place

That made you close
Your heart
To receiving who you are

Am I speaking of being selfish
Ego aggrandizement, the separated self
I am not

I am talking about
Finding and honouring
The soul sense inside
The essence of who you are

I am talking about connecting

Love yourself
As though you were your child

Cherish, sooth, encourage
The sacred sense of who you are

Who you really are is wanted here
And the world needs the gift of your love.

Do You Have the Courage?

Do you have the courage,
to honour and trust
   what you love?

The places where the heart
blossoms naturally and
the soul's face
   is revealed.

Are you willing to bring
a light of accepting awareness
to the places where love
unable to flow
has you no longer sensing
   or trusting in its wisdom?

Are you choosing to cleave
to the norms of another,
the learned forms,
rather than to deeper wisdom
   as it reveals itself to you?

Yes, there is a consequence
to choosing love.
The challenges can be rigorous.
The chances for healing and delight
   profound.

And there is a consequence
to refusing,
the heart seems to shrivel.
There is a sense of something
being lost. Of the soul
     going into hiding.

Who and what you love,
your soul's purpose and joy,
though constantly unfolding,
     are very specific.

It is only, it seems,
by honouring this specificity
that the heart opens readily,
generously, compassionately,
     to presence,

And the soul's gift
a rich experience of the moment,
of the everyday,
     is bestowed.

Soul-work

She called it Soul-work.
Work as an expression
of one's deepest being.
Not as a sacrifice of heart
to be of service,
but as an embodiment of love,
a cherishing of essence,
a sense of being true.
A listening to feelings,
a trusting of inner knowing
an inhabiting of one's gifts
with the understanding
that really living one's own life
is the present.
Is the one
essential act of generosity,
to offer to the world.

Heart on the Mend

You are not here
    a wise woman said
to fill the hole
    in other people's souls

Your are here
    to find the joy
in being who you are
    and expressing
what you love

You are here to find and honour
the wisdom of your heart
    the knowing of your soul

And in the presence
    of your living love
others are more likely to remember

To find and to mend
    themselves

You Can Forget

you can forget who you are
you can forget what you know
and what you love

when things are too stressful
or too painful
when demands are too many
when you've been shamed
for sharing who you are
when you are scared

when you have made up your mind
in a way
that does not match reality
you can close the door
to the wisdom of your soul
making it easy to be used
or to abuse

oh, you may be busy
your life may be full
but inside
you may be writhing
running or on empty

no longer connected
to the wisdom of the body
the sensing of the heart
you may never know
what you have lost
never know
the sweet trembling
vulnerability

of tenderness and love
the soft surging delight
of being at one

time to go slowly
and really feel your life
bringing empathy and mercy
to your pain
awareness and appreciation to your joy
a willingness to listen
and recognise the essential
will be needed

if you are to remember
who you are

Live What You Love

Behind the counter
At the laundry
A woman
Sorting washing.

She looks at me
With my big bundle
And beams
Till her smile
Illuminates my life.

"You've a lovely lot there,
So good of you to bring it
I love doing laundry
There's nothing in the world
I'd rather do."

Happily I leave
My curtains to her tending
And find myself in thinking

Live what you love
And you will have a smile
To light the sky.

An Unacknowledged Grief

She said she was exhausted
From doing
What she did not want
To do

This may sound like nothing
And yet the cost is huge
Of not living what we love

Even making the best
Of a bad situation
Is still staying
In a bad situation

Even when it's what
We chose to do
It's still exhausting

An oft
Unacknowledged grief

Depleting to the being
And threatening to the welfare
Of body, heart and mind.

Lay Your Burden Down

She said she was so tired
Of pleasing other people
Sensing it her job
To meet their expectation
And their need
As if the very flame
Of their soul
Depended on her
To be ignited.

She said she was exhausted
From the carrying of other persons
From believing they, or she,
Would not survive
If she did not.

Time to lay that burden down

Like the moose in the story of old
Who was so tired
Of carrying forest creatures
In his crown. Keeping them away
From the cold and sodden ground
That they might come to love him.

Then one day
With the shedding of his antlers
He set them down.
They were free to live on earth
And he was free to be.

Whenever we are sourced
In upholding other people,
We are taking them on board.

Whenever we are sourced
In communion with the essence
Of ourselves
We are setting others free
To live their lives
And ourselves
Free to be.

Natural Beauty

There is a natural beauty
and a grace
in helping one another.
In supporting those we love
or those in need.

There is a natural generosity
to the heart.
It wants to share and be supportive,
to give and to receive.

We need one another.
And we thrive when it's safe,
and mutually desired,
to be connected.

When in Doubt

Listen to your hesitation.
Often there's a wisdom
Hidden in that subtle sense
Of no.

To doubt the soul
Can be a ravage.
To doubt
The machinations of the mind
Can be a gift.

Many Are the Voices

Many are the voices
Of those
Who may seek
To control you.

Many, whose voices,
Whether yours
Or another's, that may try
To raid the heart.
To violate, shame, manipulate
Or threaten you.

Many that will hound
And keep you driven
To appease them.

Many are the voices of those
Who will promise

"I will keep you safe
But only if you are 'good' "
Obedient to my needs.

One thing to know
There will always be
"Good" reasons
Not to honour
Your own energy
Wisdom and flow.
Nor take the time

To open your heart
To tenderness
And watch if flower.

Another thing to know
Any voice
That unable to be still,
To offer mercy,
Or greet you
With kindness and compassion
Is a voice of pain
Defensiveness or fear.

Heartless in essence
This is not the voice
To soothe the soul.

That voice is sourced
In something deeper.

In something wiser

And more true
To you.

The Call

The call comes
when you do not want it.
Sometimes you know
you must go.
But sometimes
every cell in your body cries
no!

This is not
what you yearned for.
This is not the life
you imagined in that quiet
corner of your heart
where everything is known.

You sit on the edge of the bed,
your hand hovers reluctantly
over the phone.
What will you say when they ask you
as you know they will if
you call them back?

Your mouth is dry
as a drought in winter
when no one knows
if it will ever rain again.
Any more than you know
if you answer the way
you think you should

whether you will ever feel
fully alive again.

You sit praying for a downpour
and somewhere inside
a tiny voice patters:

Every sacrifice
that causes you to close
your heart,
to turn away
from the softly whispered
wisdom of your core

is a sacrifice of soul.

And there
on the edge of the bed
hand hovering over the phone
you ask yourself

are you still willing
to pay the old price?

The Time Has Come

The time has come to take back your life
From all those who would not have
That you have it.
From those who feel threatened
By your wild grace.

Those who would have you smaller
Than you are to meet their needs
Or bigger than you are to meet their demands.
Those who would threaten
Scare or cajole you into a life
You do not want.

The time has come to take back your life
From those places inside
That would seek to diminish
Or inflate who you are.
That would sever your sense of connection
To your soul and the divine.
That would refuse to see
Your blossoming beauty
Or embrace you with mercy in your pain.

The time has come to take back your life
From all whom would seek to erode your trust
In the tender moments of connection
Erode your trust in vulnerability and love,
And the unfolding wisdom of existence,
As it reveals itself
To you.

Yes, the time has come to take back your life.

Not as an act of violence, but as an act
Of surrender to compassion.

What Is It?

The old woman stood
on the snow-covered
dock, staring
after her husband
chugging his way,
in a small wooden boat,
across the smooth
pearly surface of the sea
towards his favourite spot
to fish.

Far above him
a fish eagle flew,
with the late
northern dawn,
a soaring presence
buoyed by an updraft.

The woman
pointed to the bird
and then turned to me
where I stood shivering
beside her, stamping my feet
to ward off the cold.

That bird loves to fly
she said
just as my husband

loves to fish.
They would do
nothing less.

Head cocked towards me,
eyes burning bright
as if to warm my very soul,
she asked, as I now ask you:

What is it you
essentially
came here
to do?

The Flower That You Are

The time may come
When all you want to do
Is be
The flower that you are.

No more pruning or pretending,
Bending out of shape,
Or forcing blossoms
Out of season.

One day you might find
That in the place that suits you
Your heart will open naturally
And offer all its beauty to the sky.

And all you want to do
Is be
In that place,
Surrender to the seasons
And let your life unfold.

Yes, the time may come
When all you want to do
Is be
The flower that you are.

Moon out of Bounds

*Poems of insecurity and descent.
Of honouring lunar aspects
of ourselves.*

Moon out of Bounds

I read today the moon
is out of bounds
circling the planet
outside the planes
of earth's orbit
round the sun

I read emotions
are unruly, sensitive
to extreme
security feels threatened
we are placed on shifting sands

even the solid presence
of the earth
as we have known it
no longer seems assured

there is a need
for stillness
retreat to stabilise
reconnect with my core
and return

to a place of openness
and trust in existence
as it reveals itself to me

A Time for Retreat

There is a time for retreat
For respite, rest and recuperation.

A time to withdraw
From expectations and demands
Others may be making.

There is a time
To say no
To those characters within
That would ravage
What a deeper part of us
knows, or is seeking.

There's a time for being accepting,
Tolerant and forgiving,
With feeling at a loss
Angry, frightened and confused,
Grieving, or in a mood.

There is a time for descent,
For digging down and delving
In search of something vital
Hidden in the deep.

Yes, there is a time
For retreat.

For waiting patiently
For insight to arise
And essence to unfold.

In Praise of Acceptance

There is a freedom
to be found
in acceptance.

In simply
bringing awareness
to the way things are.

Did I say resignation?
Or putting up with things?
I did not.

All I said was
a willingness to be
with things the way they are.

Precisely to give name
to what actually is so
without judgment.

I am amazed
by the freedom to be found
in acceptance.

Be Happy?

There is a certain sort of tyranny
To the thought
I should be happy.
I must feel right and be resolved,
Like some mathematical equation
Or at least seem to be OK.

There is a certain sort of shame
In feeling wretched, grieving, uncertain
Or at a loss. Being weak, or defeated.

There is little tolerance for being
Patient. Taking time to mend, ponder
Or invite insight to arise.

Any implication
That one way of being
Is better than another, might fail
To recognise the strange wisdom
In our grief, or in the simple need to be
With life as it is, and trust the mystery.

Every symptom is a sign of soul's journey

A cry for mercy. A call to love
For us to follow and embody as life unfolds.

A Welcome Present

There is no greater agitation
Than being pulled
Out of my own life

It's not so easy to return

To land in that place
Of communion and trust
In my process and my flow

There is an easing to the spirit
In dropping out
Of the worries of the mind
In returning to the wisdom
Of the heart
The knowing of the body
The experience of the being

In returning to that simple trust
In existence and its seasons
In letting life take its time

In bidding welcome to the present.

On the Right Track

So interesting to see
how life
seems to falter,
how feelings of tension
and fear, have me cowering
and fraught,
when I am not
on the right track
with myself
when I am not
honouring my soul's purpose
      and unfolding

How interesting to see
how life seems to flow,
how feelings of ease
and delight seem to flower,
when I am

When

When something
is wrong
one feels
to turn away.

When something
is right
one feels
to turn towards it
like a flower
to the sun.

Falling Down

We try so hard
To stay up
To keep from falling down
Yet there is a falling
Into ourselves
That is of the essence.

There is a tumbling
Into the heart
That means we must open
To our beauty and our pain.

Without a willingness
To surrender
To a flow of feelings
Receive them with compassion
We may never come to know
That sweet sense
Of oneness with ourselves
That simple bliss
In being
Beneath all our distress.

Without a willingness
To surrender
And turn attention
To the quiet
That underlies the turmoil

Of the mind
We may never come to know
That sweet sense
Of oneness
With existence
That sweet sense
Of love and trust and flow.

We try so hard to stay up
Yet there is a falling down
That is of the essence.

Oh To Be Understood

Most everyone wants
To be understood

Is this then the gift
You might offer
Yourself
In the night
When shadows run cold
Across the wall of your heart
When memories
Come to taunt you unbidden
With feelings of loss, guilt
Regret and shame?

Is this then the gift
To console you
In that moment of worry
And fear
When doubting
What you know and love
Speaks of self-hatred
And you no longer know
What you want
Or who you are?

Will comprehension come
When you hear yourself cry
But this is not my life

Will it fire the longing
Harnessed beneath
That quiet desperation?

Will it bring ease
To your suffering
Compassion to others
Caught writhing on the hook
Of a life not their own?

Will you weep
Finally to feel existence?

Will you kiss the tears
And realise your life?

Circle of Forgiveness

Staying in the present
With forgiveness

Forgiving me
For what I said
Or did not say
For what I did
Or did not do
For what I felt
Or did not feel

Forgiving you
For what you said
Or did not say
For what you did
Or did not do
For what you felt
Or did not feel

Forgiving me
Forgiving you
Forgiving…

Surrendering to peace
In a circle of forgiveness

Determined Gentleness

Choose kindliness
    when you can

Most of us are struggling
have places where we suffer
    no matter the face we show the world

The willingness
to set boundaries with those
who wittingly or otherwise
would seek to abuse
    is an act of compassion

A kind look or word
    is an act of grace

What Would It Be Like?

What would it be like
To let go
All the expectations and demands
We place on each other
And ourselves?

What would it be like
To let go all the guilts and shoulds?

Undo the holding on?

What would it be like
No longer to be interested
In shame?

In shaming one another?

Or using all our energy to defend
Against the coat of pain
That so often hides
The beauty and the wisdom
Of our core?

What would it be like
To be sourced in inner knowing
In that tender vulnerability
Connectedness, joy and love?

What would it be like
Not to harden in defence
But rather to surrender and release
The gift of soul?

What would it be like
To soften
Into ourselves and one another?

What To Do?

The rain came hammering
Down and down and down
It beat on the land,
The roofs, the roads

It filled the rivers
And the seas
Till waters rose
In streets and homes

She stood on the stairs
To the cellar
And watched the water rising

Shock, fear and anger
Coursed her body

What to do?

Sitting on the stairs
She wept
This was just too much!

Connecting
With a flow of feeling
She added salty tears
To all the wet

Finally she rose and knew
What she would to do

She would call a trusted friend
And ask for help

Feel first and then act
Is what she later said

The words struck a chord

Don't try to act
Whilst in the throes
Of emotion

With a patient tender presence
Bring consciousness to feeling
Allowing turbulence to flow

With merciful understanding
Wait
For inner seas to clear
That wisdom might emerge
And reveal itself to you.

Inspired with gratitude by insights and experiences shared by Cheryl Richardson in her newsletter.
www.cherylrichardson.com

There Is Nothing Like a Friend

There is nothing like a friend.
In this moment of distress
Of feeling anxious,
Not knowing what to do,
She heard me.

With such deep listening
In her heart
She let me tell my tale.

And in the telling,
Her tender presence and reflection,
Helped me remember feelings
Founding all that worry,
And reconsider notions,
Linked with them.

Tears flowed,
As is there wont,
With this presence of myself,
And a new sense of serenity arose.

No, there is nothing like a friend.

She helps me reconnect
With the sacred, silent pulse of life

                        And be restored.

Crone

Sitting by the mirror
In the health club
A woman
Dressed in black
Combing out her hair
That long silver mass
Flowing
Like a moonlit river
To well
Beyond her waist

Holding a handful
In her lap
She sat racking through it
Working out the knots
Untangling the snarls
Straightening the strands
Clearing karmic streams

With a steady, soothing hand
She took me to a realm
Where the presence
And the beauty
Of an elder is essential.

Moon Woman

Moon Woman
receives, senses, listens
refines, reflects, reveals
and retreats.

She soothes,
as she follows her path.
Offers wisdom,
as escorted by the stars,
she adheres to her rhythms
and her seasons. No wound,
nor grace, does she counter
with her forgiving light.

Hearts soften in her silvery glow.
Minds cease their endless chattering.
Relieved spirit dances
when she pours compassion
into persons parched and thirsting
for her tender light.

Without her
we would never know
who we are, or what we love.

Without her
essence would not be revealed.
And we would never know the present
that would quench our deepest thirst.
Moon Woman
holds a secret source within.

Part in shadow she weaves mysteries
no one sees. Her deepest communion
often when she is dark.
When she has turned away
to retrieve the hidden magic
of her soul.
Or make ready
to respond, when the calling
comes, to receive, reflect, and unfold
the essential.

Moon woman feels, hears, sees
distils, muses, mirrors

and moves on.

Woman in Winter

Poems of a journey through winter.
Of being in transition,
of opening to feelings
and the creative process,
of finding and cherishing the family
within.

Being in Winter

So delicate, so tender
These January days
Of fine snow falling
On trees standing stark
Dark lines drawn
Against a white sky

Light is slowly
Returning to the land
Yet little seeds held
In the earth are sleeping
Still, waiting for warmth
To return

Everything tranquil and quiet
Life pared down to the essential

Hot tea by the fire
Candles aglow

Such sweet relief
In taking this time
For soul to unfold

Like some small seed
Encouraged by warmth
And soft light to remember
Itself for all the cold
And start reaching
For the sky

Winter Heart

The lily pond is frozen
And covered with snow

Straight line tracks
Of a fox
Cross the surface
Evidence life passing

Meanwhile the lotus flowers
In winter retreat
Refuse to show their faces

Curled and sleeping
They rest
Replenishing in the deep

                Where the water still flows

Not Enough Ink

Is there time to forge
a poem upon the page
with the pen running out
of ink, and the frost melting
quickly on the land?

I want to run
on the crisp white surface
of the grass,
leave footprints to linger
on the lawn before time,
like this ink, runs out.

How easy it is
not to fill the pen with ink.
Not to dance through a morning
all a-sparkle.

The thrust of agendas
some other part of me determined
would consume me completely
if I would let them.

And soul would never leave its mark
Not even for a moment.

Anxious and Forsaken

Fingers freezing as
They clutch the pen

A shaft of sun
On frosty ground
Brings no warmth
And soon is lost
To cloud

A trip to town
Forthcoming
Energy rallies
Out of nowhere

Too rushed today
To write or feel
A thing

When the mind is
On the move
Whirling
Round its business
The heart waits tense
Anxious and forsaken

Skater in the Mist

The snow has stopped falling.
A thin white mist is on the rise,
hiding the frozen inlet like a veil.

The inlet looks strange –
cloud undulates eerily above it.
A rainbow forms in a crack
as the fog opens briefly like a curtain,
to reveal a black-clad skater
racing silently
across the surface of the sound.

Just as suddenly, she is gone,
disappearing back
into the fog, without a trace.

How elusive a sense
inspiration can be.
How it can come
and go
like a skater in the mist.

Had I not chosen to be still,
to sit and wait by the window
I would not have seen her.
And the present
would not have been
received.

Tender Relating

It has snowed again overnight.
Several inches deep, it lies
mounded over fence posts,
balanced precariously
on thin branches of trees,
and continues to fall silently
through the still air.

We must go for a walk
my beloved and I.
The path is beckoning.

We plan to walk up the hill first
have it behind us.
But coming to the hill we see
a clutch of neighbours chatting.
Preferring stillness on this day
we turn to the left instead.

In a moment, two delicate deer
prance lightly, through veils of snow,
across the road before us.

Young, unsteady on their legs,
shy and elusive, like soul seems to be,
they turn to face us, eyes alert,
ready for flight in an instant.

We stand communing
for a fragment of time.
It seems they have a message.

Be gentle with yourselves
tender and forgiving.
Stay connected to your heart place.
A tender heart is a fragile thing.

With its presence you'll be blessed
with warmth and grace and love.
But it will retreat in a moment
if you do not tend it well.
And the magic will be gone.

Yes be sensitive to yourselves
and one another
and we will come…in the quiet
when defences are all down
and you feel safe
to dance a simple dance,
of freedom, grace and of love.

Deeply moved we wander on
through untracked snow.

How finely tuned and receptive
life calls us to be…

How tenderly
we are invited to relate.

Return to Innocence

Walking down the lane
with snow falling softly
on my face
I turn towards myself
as though
I were my child.

An image comes,
not as reverie
but as insight,
of a small girl
sheltered by a wall
at the bottom of a field.

It is snowing there too,
the flakes landing softly
on her face.

I see the black of trees,
white-lined, against the snow.
The only mark across the field
her small dark footprints
along the hedgerow
leading to the wall.

Peering across it
she sees a calf,
its breath steaming
from its nostrils,

its eyes soft and brown
with a scattering of flakes
lingering on the lashes.
Its mother a distant figure
looming through the flurries,
and the calf galloping to the cow,
glad finally to suckle her warm udder.

I picture that small girl
running home
through the snow to write.

She has to write a story
about a cow and calf.

Outdoor clothes discarded,
she settles at the table,
the round one in the kitchen,
whist her mother makes her tea.

The stub of pencil,
the one with a well-chewed end,
held tightly in her hand,
hovers above the empty page
as she struggles
to find a way in to the story.

Finally she begins:

"There once was a calf
who got lost in the snow."

Then all the words come
tumbling, till she has a story
to proudly show her mum.

Coming home myself,
a short while later,
I discard my outer gear,
pop the kettle on
and settle at the table,
the round one in the kitchen.

I simply have to write.

The pen, the black one
with the golden nib,
held lightly in my hand,
hovers above the page
till I find the right words
with which to begin.

How wise the insights
of the child.
How she knows what I love.

Do you know
what is precious
to the child within?

Or have you lost it to a world
that wanted something else?

Have you suppressed
your wild longing,
deep inside?

Have you given it
away?

Do you seek it
day by day?

Are you ready to remember
and return, to innocence?

Time to Reconnect

there is
this sweet sense
of a return
to tenderness
to innocence
to love

this the gift in being vulnerable
in being brought down
by slight unwellness
time to reconnect with the magic
inner child

how easy to forgo
this simple treasure
to lose the gift
of her
to fear and agitation
the worries of the mind

there is a simple sense
of love and joy
in being present
to the child

this really is the task now
to honour and protect
her simple beauty

help bring her ease
as I live into her wisdom
and honour what she loves

when my inner child is happy
I am happy too

Inner Children

A new kind of peace
Reigns inside
When I am connected
To my inner soul child

When I find myself devoted
To noticing how she feels
Attending to her sorrows
And her joys
Honouring what she loves

A new kind of peace
Reigns inside
When I am willing to give name
To the pain
Of my wounded child within
The ways she was hurt
And is still hurting

She needs me to soothe her
When she gets scared
And re-enacts
What she has learned

Vigilant and dear
She has chosen all along
To do her best to keep me safe.

A new kind of peace
Reigns inside
When I am willing
To be present
With my inner children,
Welcoming and treasuring them both.

And it is to the innocence
And wisdom of my soul child,
I must turn
If I want to be present.

Be connected to the current
And live a life sourced in the grace
Of being at one
With her.

Family Within

Cherishing the feminine is being receptive.
Cherishing
    The maiden, mother, crone
    The sensing
    The listening
    The understanding
    The empathetic
    The reflective
    The introspective
    The knowing
    The intuitive
    The wise
    The nourishing
    The containing
    The soothing
    The processing
    The seasonal
    The cyclical
    The lunar
    The dark
    The organic
    The inclusive
    The united
    The relational
    The merged
    The body
    The in breath
    The egg
    The round

The…
Healing
    The places where she is hurting.
    Where as shadow of herself
    She devolves to distortion,
    Smothering and manipulation.

Freeing
    Her gifted grace,
    Where it has been restrained.
Trusting
    The unfolding of the feminine.

Cherishing the masculine is being expressive.
Cherishing
    The apprentice, practitioner, sage
    The outward-going
    The goal-oriented
    The measured
    The directed
    The focused
    The strategic
    The single-minded
    The contrived
    The mental
    The conceptual
    The analytical
    The structured
    The thought
    The planned
    The separating

    The differentiating
    The piercing
    The thrusting
    The solar
    The sharp
    The out breath
    The sperm
    The straight
    The...
Encouraging him in being bright
    Rather than as shadow of himself
    Using his skills to shame
    Violate, dominate and maim,
    Instead of to sustain
    The sacred gift of living.
Supporting
    Him in being competent.
    In developing his skills
    That he might use them to express
    What the wise woman knows
    And the essential soul child loves.
Affirming
    The development of his talent.

Cherishing the soul child is being essential.
Cherishing
    The authentic
    The unique
    The connected
    The integral
    The innocent

    The radiant
    The divine
    The open
    The creative
    The responsive
    The alive
    The vulnerable
    The tender
    The feeling
    The sensitive
    The spontaneous
    The emotional
    The playful
    The pure
    The…
Holding
    The child with compassion
    Tending its wounds.
    Unravelling him or her from the grip
    Of old pain and patterns of survival.
Learning
    to recognise the one who holds the soul
    from one who holds old hurting.
Trusting the soul child who knows
    Who I am
    And what I love.

Cherishing integrity is being whole
Marrying
    The feminine to the masculine
    That they might treasure one another

And receive and express the essential.

Choosing to forge a family
    That is encouraging
For woman, man and child.

In Transition

The swans of summer
have gone now,
out to open ocean,
for here the world is frozen.

Everything snow-covered,
dazzling, white. Yet my heart,
immured by an impending journey,
has been closed to all this beauty.

Psyche is keeping busy
knowing
we are on the threshold
of a return to another land.
She is building energetic bridges
to carry me across
a wild and tossing sea.

Platforms of remembered scenes
intertwined with imagined prospects
are being structured to support me.
I am already partly there.

Quietly, insistent Psyche does her work.
All I can do is let her.

Back to This Land

I've come back to this land,
where I once lived
for so long.

The re-entry seems a little rough.
The town by the airport
ugly and unloved
beset with crumbling houses.
The tunnel to the city, jammed
with fumes and honking traffic.

I cannot help but wonder
was I really right to come?

A dilapidated taxi
smelling of sweat and cigarettes
bounces me about.

Once through the tunnel
slushy streets wet with rain
slow rush-hour traffic to a crawl.

I am glad to cross the bridge
that will bring me home.

Glad to be driven
beneath bare winter trees,
and see the white city geese
pad about the edge
of the river's frozen form.

It makes me sad their wings are clipped.
I imagine they longingly look up
when wild geese
fly overhead.
Though in reality I wonder if they notice.

Home at last there is sanctuary.

My eyes light upon a painting of angels.
They appear all a-flutter with the flicker of the candles.

The soft touch of wings, seem to brush against me.

A soothing end to a journey
I did not want, yet trusted all the same
was essential.

Cellular Shock

Tiredness
has been stalking
like a shadow
in the night.
Invisible yet
always
always there.
As body
does its thing
to adjust,
and let me
be,
here in this place
where almost all
shapes and sensations
seem somehow strange.
In this place
where my cells
crave the peace,
to recover the shock
of sudden flight,
from one collective
to another.
From one consciousness
to the other.

False Light

I sit in my bed
with a cup
of pre-dawn
tea
searching
for a place
to begin

Hard
in all this
false city
light
to find
the subtle
luminosity
of soul

Hard
in this place
that has
so little tolerance
for darkness

City Rose

I think of the rose
Withered
In winter retreat
Dreaming of a spring
Where she might blossom
And offer up her fragrance
To the world.

I think of that longing
For water, for light
For rich earth
To nourish her roots,
As I stand
On tarmacadamed ground

In a city
That offers little
To that flower,
Cut back and dried,
Other than a small pot
In which to live.

An Ancient Issue

A cold winter's day,
following a solar eclipse.

I yearn to be
quietly with the writing,
but it hasn't been flowing.
An ancient issue
has obscured my heart instead.

I've been dealing
yet again
with the old shaming voice
of the wizened one within.
The one who, ever critical,
shrivels life and withers love,
with a look or word.

Different from a mean
matriarchal voice who feels
she must manipulate,
and withhold love to control,
this voice claims its power
by making people wrong.

Honed by eons
of hard, cold utterances
from a ruler to a ruled,
and whetted
by centuries of being disgraced,

whenever something tender
showed its face,
this is a patriarchal voice
of pain and shame
handed down over the years
from an adult to a child,
and in certain forms of hierarchy.

I have had the sensation
ever since the moon crossed the sun,
that this voice inside myself
felt itself eclipsed,
and now wants an old revenge.

So I shiver in my shoes.
Too many times before
I have been inveighed
for loving what I love,
frozen in my tracks,
by a searing look or a word,
scorched in my heart place,
by a sudden flare.

Oh no, not again,
not on this day
of fresh snow sparkling
on the ground.

On this day I shall recognise
that voice for what it is:
an old hurt place within.

An acquired source of influence
I once thought I must depend on
to survive.

On this day,
of the moon having slid
across the sun, I shall
send that voice compassion
for its pain

and chose to say hello
to something more essential
than the wizened one within.

Glamour of the Shield

And so comes the question,
how best to cherish the heart's unfolding?
How best to protect it?

Surely not by becoming like a fortress,
or by shutting down?

Surely not by building up an armoury
or assuming battle garb?

Even though some do seem alluring.
And some who chose to wear them seem
so charismatic, and bear a certain sort of glory.

Too many times before what was real,
what the heart knew and loved, was lost
to the glamour of a shield,
to mental machinations and manoeuvres
of attack and defence.

Too many times before the ability
of waiting for wisdom to arise was lost
to the allure of the aegis.

NO!!! Even though I still may don them,
I don't want to become good at bearing suits of mail.

Not after all these years of longing – of working –
for those old suits to soften,
for my battle dress to crack or melt
that love might shine right through.

For love after all is
the best defence.

Hidden from View

Worries have been plaguing me for days.
Gnawing at my heart, they stop
the writing that I love.

Sloshing down the street
through mounds of slush and grim,
the hem of my long coat drags sadly
with the weight of it all.
It flaps sodden round my legs,
as a mean little mizzle fuzzes
hair and face.

I am glad to come home.
Glad the day is ending.

But, that night, even though the sky is bright,
I cannot find the moon.
Its face,
suffused with sad city light bouncing off cloud,
is hidden from view, just like my heart.

Snuggled on the sofa,
I ask my heart, where it has gone.
It replies with an image, of a child at school,
hauled in front of class to read an essay.

And oh, the teacher was so cross
This was not the kind of essay she had expected.
"This is all in your imagination," is what she said.
"You don't come to school to be imaginative.
You come to school to learn. What I want to teach you."

Picturing that scene makes me cry.
Hot tears run down my face.

Oh, how that old critical voice
housed within myself and others,
has been able to suppress
my passion and my joy.

How I have succumbed
and forgotten
that any endeavour of the heart
is bound to bring a chance
to clear old emotional debris.

So this is just another one of those.
Another chance to see
what is standing in between
my love and me.

The following morning I am again
brought home to the writing.

Opening the curtains before settling down,
I am strangely comforted to see
the earth
has revealed itself again
between old banks of snow.

And that there, in a warm little corner
with a cushion of white behind it,
stands the first fragile snowdrop of the year.

Damp Wood on the Fire

A slow Saturday afternoon.
Rain.
Damp wood on the fire.

Snowdrops no longer covered in snow.
Their little heads wobbling instead with wet.
Long lines of droplets on twiglets on trees
And me marching along
Wondering yet again about the writing.

What a process this has been.
How wobbly thoughts have plagued me!
How they have been able to suppress
My wildest dreams.

No! I do not want this.
Do not want to be defined
By ideas that are too small
For my passion,
Too confining for my heart.

Rain bounces off the rim of my hat
Sprinkling my cheeks.
I wipe the cold little droplets away
And find myself wondering yet again
How best to honour and to shield
What is precious deep inside?

It seems that being kindly
And compassionate holds a key –
Patient and forgiving,
Alert to my process.

I imagine myself dancing
Beneath an umbrella
Of kindness, and compassion
And soon find myself back home.

Yes, oh yes, to be home.
It was inspiring to be out,
Now it is inspiring to be in.

With the curtains drawn
And fire rekindled,
I start to write
About inhabiting my life.

It seems to require such fortitude and faith
In a world that always seems so greedy
For something more, or else.

Last Remnant of the Rain

The sun has come out
and this along with the breeze
is chasing the last remnant
of the rain
away.

Small sparkling droplets
are scattered along fences, caught
on bushes, and are held
on old grasses and reeds.

And there, in its warm little corner
stands that first fragile snowdrop
of the year

its petals opened out like
an umbrella...

The Smallest Thing

Today this almost numinous sense
of gratitude for life.

The smallest thing seems to bring joy.

A tiny bird all puffed up and fluffy
perched on a branch beyond the window.

A small snowdrop standing fragile
on moist earth bathed in sunlight.

A simple choice, of choosing to rest,
when feeling vulnerable and tired...

How often, the most exquisite moments
come when I am my least defended.

It's so easy to seek myself, or life, ambitiously,
devise regimes, formulas and techniques,
all in a search of a sense of connection, presence,
or joy.

Yet sometimes doing nothing is
the most fruitful task of all.

Winter Swans

The swans are back now
Home from their winter sojourn
Out at open sea.

Strong in their desire
To make a nest a
And hatch their young,
Just as they were strong
In their heading out,
They are here
Flying long and low
Searching
The still frozen inlet
For the odd patch
Of water
On which to land.

Spying a small puddle
Softened by the thaw
They arrive with a splash.

There they sit
Resting before running,
Great black feet
Slipping on the solid surface
Of the sea
As, with a flapping fanfare
Of wings,
They launch themselves
Skyward yet again.

How hard it can be
To return. To settle
In a still barren land.

How hard to trust the calling
When there was grief
To the leaving
In the first place.

Just as there is grief
In saying goodbye
To the heaving ocean
That once offered sustenance,
If not a home, to those wild,
White winter swans.

Song of the Inlet

Standing in the snow
hearing
the frozen inlet sing.

The slowly shifting
cracking ice
calls out
like an ancient whale
from the depths.

Its long echoing yowl,
such a primordial sound,
resonates with something deep.

Calling me to listen and remember:
that tracking feelings
with acceptance and awareness,
changing my mind,
when my way of thinking isn't true,
though invisible work
has value just the same.

Yes, the song of the inlet
beckons me this day,
to treasure and to trust
the deep
inner-sea navigation
that helps me find
and follow the essential.

Edge of Spring

Now, after the lunar eclipse
    With midnight's full red moon
        Shining down
            On slow retreating snow
Come the tears

Grief is the way we complete things
    Someone said

So I will wash away the ache
    Of winter's undertaking

And turn my face,
    Like some small faithful flower
        Found hidden in melting snow
Towards the light again

Woman in Summer

Poems of a journey through summer.
Of finding new ways of relating,
of letting go and trusting,
of cycles of death and rebirth.

Pure Spun Gold

A dragonfly perches
On an old grey wooden table

Reddish-brown of body
Translucent of wing,
He sparkles in the sunshine
Wrought through with little lines
Of copper and pure spun gold

A sign of transformation
It is said

Perhaps he is a herald
A sweet and small reminder
To seize the moment while we can
Bask in sunlight and transmute
Our tarnished copper into gold

Morning Reflection

Nature doesn't speak
                to me today

A swan nibbles
with desultory bites
and tugs, at the reeds,
barely moves
a still and silent sea.

A conflict unresolved
is eating at my heart.

The swan
beyond the window
                has no meaning now.

Reply to a Worried Mind

When
a new poem
is ready
it will present
itself to you

Tears of Salt

Salty tears upon the page.
Little lakes running
into inky rivers
down the paper.
No poem,
only jumbled words
since she said, "Your writing
is no good. You got it wrong.
It does not fit. Does not belong."

No poem
not a one, since she ripped
my heart apart
with her shiny steely sword.

How we hurt one another,
how we hurt ourselves,
when words become weapons
of opinion, instead of servants
of the soul.

You might think
this is nothing.
But this is serious.

There are those who spend
a lifetime never doing
or ever knowing
what they love
because they once were hurt
in their heart-place
for sharing of themselves.

Salty tears upon the paper.

Little lakes rusting memories
beliefs and ideas
formed in meetings
with steely swords.

Inky streams of words running
down the page. And a poem.

Yes, a poem
       is born.

It Is Always Like This

It is always like this
Though I tend
To forget

After a spate of grieving
Or delving in the deep
There comes a sacred gift

A new poem perhaps
A fresh joy in being

Yes, it is always like this
Even though I tend
To forget

On The Rise

Cocktail conversation swirls
All around me
I am on the up and up
Rising towards the place where I
Find myself, hoisted like some olive on a stick,
Poised precariously between being devoured by
Inconsequential chit-chat
Or being frozen by a dip in iced spirits.

Perhaps I will drop to the floor
And be trodden on by those
Who may never know
What lies underfoot.
Be crushed
On the multi-coloured carpet
Victim of some stiletto heel.

Or maybe from my lowly position
I will roll quietly across the floor
And out the door?

Ah! Yes!

Such sweet relief no longer to adapt
To strain to connect
But be on the level
With myself.

Reply to Mr Cut and Dried

We are not
Emotional islands
Standing rigid
And untouched
In a feeling sea.

We are not
Really separate.

We are live
Relational beings.
Vibrant and organic,
Responsive and reflective,
Empathetic and creative,
Real.

Everything we say
Or do
Has an impact.

Every word,
Every action
Counts.

Yes, sometime it is right
To insulate oneself
From putrid springs.
Move away from that
Which poisons.

Not to stand aloof
In the deep.
But rather
That we might meld
With the life force
Of the sea.

We are made of water
And we know
When not pretending
To be insular

Just how connected
We are.

In the Mirror

  Sometimes when I feel
  A draw to another person,
  Or a real aversion,
  When placing on a pedestal
  Or a judgment rears its head,
  It's good to stop and see.

What it is in my view
      Of the other
That is really a reflection
Of something not yet seen
      Or realised yet in me.

All They Did Was Shout

Watching two married people on TV
in the chaos of perpetual conflict
and endless shouting.

Each was demanding that the other change,
conform to his or her image
of how the other was supposed to be.

They both pointed fingers and accused
without end.
It felt like a shock,
a ravage just to watch this.
I wanted to turn my face away
but, strangely fascinated
found I could not.
I was bound to the story
in a search with these characters
for an illusive redemption that was not to come.

Two wounded hearts were holding sway
with never a moment to tarry with the tender,
or linger with compassion.
Where was the love? Where was the grace?
They were hidden
behind words that disparaged and disjoined.

Throughout the movie one could see
the vulnerable experience
of the heart being destroyed.
Each time it showed its face
it was trampled upon.

The couple were just so interested
in getting their own needs met,
in dominating one another,
there was never a moment
in which their thoughts,
actions and reactions
could be questioned and observed.

Their angry, defensive, abusive attacks
just kept on coming
along with their angry defensive,
abusive replies.
They never got to see
how harmful harsh words can be.

They never got to empathise
with themselves or one other,
be kindly or sensitive to feelings.

Never got to recognise
the true sources of their pain,
change their minds,
or be forgiving.

Though both were longing
for love, they were both
doing the very things
that would ensure
they would not get it.

Such a grief to see
two vulnerable human beings,
unique in all the universe,
choosing to be at war.

A Gift from Existence

Standing by the window
watching a black-clad couple
down by the water practising tai chi.

Their movements
beneath their billowing garb,
are so fluid and attuned,
they seem almost one.
Like some large, strange, bird
or dark dragon.

No one is the leader,
no one is the follower,
no one is the boss.
No one is demanding,
judging or controlling.

Each is left to be
complete in themselves.

Each free to be
a graceful, flowing concord.

Even when one flounders
their flow is not disturbed.

As their movements merge,
it is as if a new way of being
blossoms, like a gift, from existence.

A gift where two distinct forces
maintain their own identity
yet sometimes seem so melded
they are one
in the making of rapport between them.

Mutuality Is Round

Explorers of consciousness is what we may be, often beavering quietly unfolding new forms, expressing new ways of creating connection without violation, finding new ways of relating with heart, and of inhabiting mutuality.

I was musing with a friend
about the possibility
of moving from hierarchy,
a way of relating in which people
or elements are ranked,
towards mutuality,
a way of relating
that does not require
the dominion of one
over the other,
but rather invites us
to let ourselves
and each other be.

Invites us to make
emotional safety
for ourselves and each other,
that creativity, compassion and kindness
might flower, and wisdom unfurl.

We found ourselves wondering
could this be a time
imbued with strands of possibility
for realising mutuality?

Indeed we even wondered
if evolution might be trying
something here?
If it might be calling for a move
from patriarchy to partnership?

Not that I know well
how to do this.
More that I am wanting
to feel into the terrain here.

Oh! I am feeling a need
to endeavour to be clear,
begin exploring a territory
we might travel together,
if you want to come?

Could this be a time
of opening hearts?
Of inviting empathy for
ourselves and each other?
Of deepening awareness
of varying needs,
giving space for difference,
of finding ways of
agreeing peacefully
to disagree?

A time of delving,
alone or together,
to uncover deeper meaning,

and connect
with a sound place inside
ourselves and each other?

Could this be a time
of changing minds
of finding ways to
express
freedom and love,
cherish integrity
our own and each other's?

A time of including our hearts
as well as our minds,
our bodies
as well as our souls
and build intimacy
where intimacy is desired?

It seems to me to take heart
as well as awareness
and plenty of compassion
to inhabit our lives.
To encounter the loneliness
and pain that can come
in being genuine
and not shutting down.
Not shutting down to the joy
that can come or the grief
or the longing…

It seems to me to take heart,
mind, body and soul,
to dwell in relationship,
to unfold that mystery
that sorrow, that wonder,
that delight...
for the dance of mutuality
to unfold.

For unlike the pyramid of hierarchy,
mutuality is organic
and round.

*Written after watching Dr Christiane Northrup on TV
speaking of moving from patriarchy to partnership*

In a Small Circle

A group of women gather
in a small circle.

They sip tea, talk a while
then change awareness
by being still.

When moved to speak,
they seek to voice
the depths of experience,
tap in
to current life unfolding.

They listen deeply
and receive
their own, and one another's
worlds.
They hold them with compassion
as best they can,
and do not try to fix
or change things.

Extending a gentle invitation
for awareness
they give space
for different views
and for their own view
to evolve.

They choose to dialogue,
    connect with a flow of meaning
rather than debate argue, or try to win
    by enforcing one idea over another.

In the act of speaking,
when there is sanctuary
for soul,
they hear themselves saying
things previously unknown.

They are together in moments
of soundless presence too.
New meaning or support often comes
as they delve for the gold at the heart
of any matter.

Delving, that delicate art,
involves a passionate practice
of inquiry
that threads their time together.

And so the women speak
and are heard, are silent
and are understood.
Soul is furthered
simply by their being
together.

When they feel complete,
that everything
that needs to be said,
has been said,
they thank one another
hug,
and head for home.

Sea of Consciousness

There is just nothing
like being together
in service of soul
in being present
to that

invitation for insight
and wisdom
to arise

that listening and sharing
mirroring and holding
that hearts and minds
might open
in a mutual sea of consciousness
and connect

No, there is just nothing
like being present
to souls
unfolding

Although You Are Gone

Although you are gone
You are not gone

You are here
In the shiny halo round the palms

In the silver flutter
Of the willows

In the white candles on the chestnut,
Its branches bowing
With the breeze

You are here
In the golden glow across the land

In the starlight dancing
On the waves

In small fish who like
To jump through the surface
Of the sea

You are here
In the tiny bird
Singing
Its sacred song

And in the wisdom
Of your words
Still whispered
In my ear

You are here
In the tender blanket
Love sometimes likes to wrap
Around me

For although you are gone
You are not gone

Sacrifice

Red apples holding
Onto the tree in the wind
Not wanting to let go
Bounce on the ground
Be bruised, even smashed
Before, if they're lucky,
Being consumed.

Oh they were made
For this
Designed to be eaten
By the deer
Who will come,
When the world is still,
Lift them from the ground
In their soft-lipped mouths
And devour them.

The seed however
Cries out
For this strange journey
To be transported
To some fresh and fertile patch
Merge with the earth, crack
And release the small tree
Hidden inside it.

For every birth
Some kind of death
Some kind of surrender
Of what went before
Yet to refuse this dying
Is a sacrifice too.

Those apples
Still clinging to the tree
When winter comes
May rot away uneaten
And their shrivelled seeds
Will fall
Too close to the mother tree
To blossom.

Black

I am vulnerable now.
My inner cadence a trembling
assailable blue.
Grief comes in waves.
I have fallen
in a sea of sorrow.

Death is a wrench.
I understand
why people want to wear black.
Want to carry some sort of sign
that soul has been shocked.

Heart is on the surface.
I am in need of tenderness.

In conversation
with my scared inner child,
I attempt reassurance.

I will be your mummy and your daddy now.

And mother earth and father sky
will watch over us.
We will be their child
tonight.

And tomorrow
I'll wear black.
I promise you,
I will.

In the Balance

A tree stands bright
Against the sky
A golden leaf
Solitary amidst the green
Flutters slowly
Toward ground

A still day today
Sun peeking out
Through cloud
Life moving slowly
Towards the fall

The thin treble of a bird
Beckons me to listen

"Nature and your nature
Have their times
They know what to do
And when,"
It seems to sing

When worlds are shifting
    Let them

Water Lily Hearts

*Poems of connecting with the present.
Of longing and belonging
of leaving and of coming home and
of remembering the heart.*

In Soft Surrender

There is a silky
Excitement
In being
Here

On the dock
With the water
Washing rocks
With little waves

And the swan
Amidst a sea
Of stars
Long neck arching
Reaching down
To feast on reeds

The love
Of this place
Has me quivering

In soft surrender
To the present

The Gift of Here

Whenever I remember
I realise
Just how in love
I am with here.

How easy
To forget
When troubles
Take me, demands
Make their mark,
Or my mind
Makes me think
Its concerns
More important
Than communing
Here, with you.

A glance
Out the window
At the swan
Fully rigged
White wings high
And pointing
On the pale
Smooth surface
Of the sea
Is enough
To remind me.

To bring me
To my knees
Yet again
In realisation
Of the gift
That is here.

Whenever I Am Away

Whenever I am away
I long
For this place

A yearning of a kind
That has me leaning
Forward
As if the very motion
Might help me
To return

Longing

Longing for home
A nourishing space
A sanctuary
                    a place

Longing for shelter
For beauty belonging
For essence reflected
                    revealed

Yes, longing
For the world
To be a place
Where soul
Knows itself
Invited
                    to reside

Longing and Belonging

There is a kind of longing
In not belonging.
In not finding mirroring
Or nourishment
In the place
We call home,
Or with the ones
We call our family
And friends.

There is a kind of longing
For belonging,
For communion
With existence, that
No one can resolve
Besides ourselves.

Even though the presence of another,
Can bring solace to the heart,
Inspiration to the mind,
Joy to the soul,
A sense of union,
We must sometimes say goodbye
To situations where we no longer flourish
Or to those
Who no longer cherish
The essence of who we are.

Sometimes it seems
We must leave home
In order to find home.

Lost in Transition

Heat envelopes us
as we step off the plane.
Modern marble halls,
monuments to travel,
echo footsteps
as we rush to claim bags.

But the small highland terrier
shivering in his cage
just goes round and round
on the carousel
and no one comes to claim him.

It seems he is forgotten
here in southern Spain
when he should have been
in France.

That small dog has stayed with me.
Lost and alone in Andalusia.

Yes I wonder about that puppy
as I ponder

how hard the toil of travel.
How costly the toll
of transition.

How terrible,
and yet how easy
it sometimes is
to lose the essential.

Cross Cultural Souls

some of us
are given
to being
cross cultural souls
no one place can contain
or sustain
us

some of us
through choice
circumstance, or love
find ourselves in places
we might not have expected
to be

and when
the pain arises
which it will,
of not belonging to the old,
not belonging to the new,
some of us are drawn
to delving
in search of essence

to finding something
deeper and more real
to depend on
than the norms
we may have learned

the expectations
we may have formed
or that others
now
may be trying
to teach us

some of us
are drawn
to find belonging
in union
with our nature

yes, some of us
are called
to the challenge
and the gift
of being
cross cultural souls

Via Negativa. Via Positiva

The Via Negativa takes you home
By bringing awareness to your No

By noticing when your heart
Does not feel drawn
When something
Doesn't feel right
Or does not seem to match
Your desires,
Your priorities
Your energy
Your wisdom
Your flow.

And through all the noticing
Of your No-ing
Emerges like a mountain
Slowly revealed
As shroud of mist lifts
A recognition of your Yes.

The Via Positiva takes you home
By bringing awareness to your Yes

By noticing where
Your heart feels drawn.
When things feel right
Or seem a match
For your desires,

Your priorities,
Your energy,
Your wisdom
Your flow.

And through all the noticing
Of your Yes
Emerges like a mountain
Slowly revealed
As a shroud mist lifts
The courage to say clearly
With much tenderness
And love

No.

To that which does not encourage
Who you are.

If You Don't Feel Safe

It's been said
If you don't feel safe
It's not your home.

How many of us do
Feel safe
Inside our homes?

How many
Feel invaded or curtailed,
Used or abused,
Or trapped inside a fortress?

How many of us feel safe
Inside ourselves?
Know the heart to be
Worthy of our trust?
A safe haven for the soul?

How many of us
Have the courage
And the willingness
To feel?
Know empathy
For ourselves
And for others?
Are able to bring
A tender light

Of awareness and compassion
To our pain?
To soften and accept
Rather than deny or defend
Ourselves against it?

Or change the stories
That we tell
When they clearly
Lack the accuracy
To bring us real relief?

How many of us
Are burdened
By unacknowledged grief?
How many free to breathe?

There is of course
No immunity to life.

There is however
A kind of quiet
Exuberant sense
Of joy
A sweet soft holding
And delight
When your heart
Becomes a trusty friend
And your house
A mirror
Of your soul.

For what they say
Is true
If you don't feel safe
Inside
Your house
It will never be
Your home —

    A place where you
        Can flourish.

Water Lily Heart

Three hearts beat inside me.
Three hearts let me know
How I feel,
And who and how I am.

Lotus-petal-like
They overlay one another
Forming a flower of experience.

One heart is wounded.
It beats with lost memories
Of old pain.
These seem determined
Just to rise up and grab me
Cloud the colour of my petals,
Even though I might wish
They would not.
Or might not realise
That my colours are no longer true.

Hurting in my soul place
It is easy for a wounded heart
To seize control. To connive
And contrive and stain my hue.
Or make me try to be a flower
That lives on land.
When in reality I am
A water lily.

One heart is wise.
It holds me cupped
In compassion.
Its many petals
Folded round my core.

Warm with understanding
This heart spoons its medicine
Through connectedness and knowing.

It brings acceptance
And awareness to my wounds.
Succour to my grief and pain.

It brings appreciation
To my love and joy,
Insight to my choices,
Presence to my life
Clarity to my colours.

Rooted in the wisdom of the deep
This heart knows I am more
Than the places I feel pain.
My old defences and denials
And the strategies I formed
To survive.

A heart that is wise
Is a sanctuary
For soul.

One heart is tender
It beats with the essence
Of my core.
It holds with my uniqueness.

Innocent, though not naïve,
Childlike though not childish,
Vulnerable and yet mature,
A tender heart is sensitive,
Natural, awake, its colours pure.

Rooted through compassion
To the deep, and held in a wise cup
Of sacred knowing
It is nourished by the dark.

Encouraged to reveal itself
When graced by loving light,
It only shows its face
When feeling safe
To be real.

Three hearts beat inside me
Colouring my life.
Water lily like
They open and close
In a dance with existence.
And in the dancing
They let me know how I feel,
And who and how I am.

Being Essential

now to living deeply
close to heart and soul
now to living gently
on the earth
as
cradled by existence
we listen for the tender
sense of essence
glimpse its touch of grace
tend its sign of beauty
foster love's embrace
in the manner of our lives

The Road Home

The road home always involves
A reclamation of the heart.
A finding and following
Of feeling. A mending
Of the places
Where we've been rent
From ourselves.
A remembering
And an honouring
Of love.

Yes, the road home always involves
A reclamation of the heart.